INDIGO SUNSHINE

Printed by BookBaby

7905 N. Crescent Blvd., Pennsauken, NJ 08110

ISBN: 978-1-66783-222-7

Dearest Reader,

Titles and epigraphs are essential to

the meaning of each poem.

Pretty please,

read them before you read the poem.

Thank you!

Lee

More than anything,
I must have flowers,
always, always.

Claude Monet

Alberta *Lee* Orcutt is an advocate for: elderly golden-agers, women & teenagers, all genders, all ancestries, the poor & destitute, erasing racism, erasing domestic violence, flower gardens, dandelions for the bees, wildlife, peace, and poetry. And she is a performance poet [a cross between stand-up comedy and a one-act play]. Lee has performed in 27 venues, including the Nuyorican Poets Café, New York City; Walker Art Center, Minneapolis; The Loft Literary Center, Mpls; Patrick's Cabaret, Mpls. She's won eight poetry awards, including the Valata Dakota Fletcher Award at UofMN; The Loft Mentor Series, Mpls; semi-finalist in both poetry & fiction in the William Faulkner international competition in New Orleans, and has had 50+ poems published in 38 print-media, including *ART-LIFE* sold by the Guggenheim, New York City.

An octogenarian, Lee was born in January 1942 in Oklahoma, a Scots-Irish-Cherokee, and at age 14 moved with her family to Minnesota. She refers to herself as a *Minnesota-Okie* and cherishes both states.

Photo by Galen Higgins

"I don't believe in aging. I believe in forever altering one's aspect to the sun."
Virginia Woolf— A Writer's Diary

KUDOS

Deepest bows to Joy Harjo, the late Lucille Clifton, Stuart Dybek, Marge Barrett, Michael D. Browne, and Anna Reckin, for their time & kind help given to a hopeless beginning poet.

Tip of my hat to N. Scott Momaday who declined my offer to be his adjunct wife. Sage decision. [Pun intended☺]

My fondest adoration for my fab family of writers the past fifteen years: Al Rieper, Bill Nemmers, Jacquie Trudeau, and Wendy Henry—our coterie of fun forever friends, helpers, confidantes.

Grandest accolades to my performance coach, the priceless, incomparable, Heidi Arneson.

My ongoing gratitude to *The Loft Literary Center* for their profound help via person-to-person exposure to literary giants, and for their insights given to the writers of the world.

Many, many thanks to each publisher of the hard-copy periodicals & books in which the following 31 poems first appeared:

A View from the Loft: E=mc², *ART-LIFE*: An Old Custom, *Close to the Ground*: Another Bloody Hysterectomy Poem, *Earth's Daughters*: Soul Food, *Fine Lines*: Garages, Gravity, Night in the City, *Minnesota Monthly*: We Have Seen the Greater Goddess, *Passaic Anthology*: I Took My Red Heart, *Paterson Literary Review*: Healing Rituals, *Perceptions*: Menopause Whorl, *Runes*: Certainty, *The Talking Stick*: At the Birdfeeder, *Writer's Exchange*: There Used to Be So Many Butterflies, *Maggie's Gift*: Gossamer, Straw Mules, Seize the Summer, Young Daughter Damon, Regarding Certain Wildflowers, Through Bramble Bushes [title change], Beauty, Sisyphia's Solution, Food & Drink [title change], Sans a Lover, A Goddess [title change], *Side-walks*: Advice, *Minnesota Women's Press*: Airborne Sex, *Passager*: Cinderella, Ostrich, *Poets On*: Pals [title change], *Imagination Within*: Mr. Ego [title change]

DEDICATION

This book is dedicated with highest esteem:

For the poets of antiquity who scythed the path for all of us

For the nine Greek muses who whisper to me

For my Ballast: My partner Bill's love, humor, support,
kindnesses & his hard work to boost funds for this endeavor
May life never let you down

For parents who upheld me with their unflagging support,
humor, empathy, and for their last-cent generosity to all

For the camaraderie of champion brother Larry

For my amazing Beloveds: Daughter Damon, son-in-law Josh,
and grandsons Otis and Wally
May all your wildest dreams come true
Thank you forever for choosing me

For Jerry & Robert who forgave me
May you and yours prosper in the spice of life

For 42 aunts and uncles and 45 first-cousins
whose positive influence is incalculable

For all my nieces and nephews
May your umbrella always open

For our five families of delightful beneficent neighbors

For friends, every single one, who listen, comfort, laugh

And for the wisdom of Winnie-the-Pooh

INDIGO SUNSHINE

ALBERTA LEE ORCUTT

NEW & SELECTED POEMS

BookBaby

Pennsauken, New Jersey

CONTENTS

MICRO

MESO

MACRO

Love is the poetry of the senses.

Honoré de Balzac

MICRO

Being poetry . . .

    lounging on the porch chaise

        listening to my apple

A goddess is
resting.

Best not make
a sound.

Cranky when wakened,
thickheaded,
she's apt to stumble and
break a bone
not her own.

———————————————

Urgh, the man in the moon
isn't the man in the moon—
The woman in the moon
Luna
Lunar
Luminate
Menses
Mystery
Stellar
Voluptuous!

FRIENDSHIP

A full moon and I see
garden shadows of two women
forehead-to-forehead
sharing a popsicle.

FASHION STATEMENT

Women who wear big
dangly silver earrings
have vivacious verve.

My aunt bought three pair
one to give to her mother
one to give to me
and one to garner men.

ON FIRE

It is said that after dark
you fantasize about
all the exotic places
where you
secretly want to be.
            —Get gussied up
            and go for it.

THE TOUCH

It hurtled through her
like honeyed rum
and she succumbed.
Plumb sated, mated.

HOTSHOT

Zeus
on the loose
in his red
Lamborghini
convertible—

You'd think he
was an only child.

SHE'S GONE

No texts.
No tweets.
Not for days and days.
Nothing.
Damn—
I'll have to buy my own
season hockey tickets.

WARNING

My heart
looks like a heart
pumps like a heart
thumps like a heart
is a heart.

Watch yourself.
This is not a toy.

SPILLED MILK

No use crying over
spilled coffee
spilled cola
spilled tea
spilled cirò.

Sob and wail over
a spilled secret.

HERE AND NOW

One brownie left
next to my empty coffee cup
—I say to myself
   I'll save it for later
as I take a bite.

Delayed gratification?
Have read about it . . .

EXERCISE

Falling down the stairs
is pretty good exercise, gets
your heart rate right up there—
the only equipment needed is one
multi-talented orthopedic surgeon.

SHEER BLISS

I yearn
for my own personal
hypotenuse,
the shortest distance
from here to any spa
—deep-tissue massage
    paradise pain

MODEST OR SHOWOFF?

Laon [Lay-uhn] France folklore:
The Peacock and the Crow
'A clever crow always paints its feathers black.'

We simply must
paint our feathers
black—
31 million
modest crows
can't be wrong.

RE: QUANTUM MECHANICS

Through rose-colored glasses
she asked PHYSICS to marry her.
He declined. Said she never
sticks to the mechanics, always
wanders off through wildflowers.

A IS FOR AGAIN

Another
Beneficent
sCrewup

WINDY

She, a cheery gust of wind,
told great jokes
never winding down.

Whatever happened to
'Did you hear the one about . . .?'

DING DONG! AVON CALLING!

Remember those teeny tiny
lipstick-tube samples? And then
our moms let us play dress-up
and we smeared red all
around our lips, remember?

Garden theft.
Rabbits harvested carrots.
It's a wonder they had time.

———————————————

After first frost
harvest Brussels sprouts
and stealthily
throw on compost pile.

RED FOX IN OUR YARD

Beautiful.
She saw me, froze darted raced down
the copse slope as I called after her,
Come back when you can stay longer!

HUBRIS

Little-Brown bat
30 years in the freezer
My show and tell

RATTLESNAKE

Diamonds
are not always
a gal's best friend.
After all,
you _were_ warned.

BRAIN WAVE

Halfway up to Mount Sandia's
peak, it dawned on me—
our cable car was built by
the lowest bidder.
What a relief.
Lowest bidders try harder.

PARTHENOGENESIS

An all-female species—
    Desert Grassland Whiptail Lizards
    You go, gals!
    Whip those super-long tails!
And oh my goodness,
such cute little baby Lizzies!

PURIM

Based on her disastrous
outcomes, she decided to
BUY her hamantaschen
rather than try yet again
to make it herself—
the better to enjoy
munching on the villain.

IRIS

Beside the worn path

>   powdery lemon center
>   gives way to courtesan's
>   wine velvet robe

Exotic caesura.

GOSSAMER

Early morning sun
glitters
on the dew-covered
spiderweb
woven on
the old wooden gate
framed in lilacs.

Into your car some morning
when you're on the freeway,
apricot moon
will cast her gaze on you alone,
command you to rise . . .

———————————————————

Rule of Chess:
Every dilemma has at least
three options from which
we can make our choice.
We must choose wisely and
Never Retreat.

FAVORITE FLOWER

Wild honeysuckle
grew beside Grandma's
torn saggy back-screen door
where I sat cross-legged on
Oklahoma overgrown crabgrass
inhaling ambrosia.
Luxury.

During the night
I am visited by the ghosts
of the world's environment
            quaking
            keening

MESO

*"Poetry and hums aren't things which you get,
they're things which get you,
and all you can do is
go where they can find you."*

Winnie-the-Pooh
The House at Pooh Corner 1928
A.A. Milne

OMAR KHAYYÁM

It takes about 70 hours to drag a poem into the light.
Mary Oliver, Blue Pastures 1995 Harcourt Brace

The hand of the poet writes
and having writ
rewrites
and does not move on
forever more:
nor all your piety nor wits
shall make it keep
that half a line
nor all your tears
prevent it from
changing a word
or two or three or more
and taking out a comma.

PENNILESS POETESS

Does anybody out there
know any guys who are
willing and able
and eager
to pay a cool hundred bucks
for a quickie poem?

If not, there's nothing to do but
shake out my 1960
pink chiffon prom dress
and head down
to the Geriatric Light District
in hopes the old codgers
can see to read a poem.

INDIGO SUNSHINE

Color is a matter of vibrations, reaching what is most
indefinable in nature—its inner power. Paul Gauguin

Life without seeing an Indigo Bunting
   is an unfinished pastoral painting

If you are singularly fortunate,
   alongside a country road
   perched on a hedgerow
   you will see splendor

Radiant lazuli blue, phosphorescent—
A zillion times bluer than other birds of blue

Bluer even
than Gauguin's wrestling angel

I WISH I HAD A CREEK

I haven't any sea in my blood,
too enormous, tempestuous.

Much better is a creek out back,
fresh clear dancing water, the

chaperone of turtles and ferns
and damsel flies and watercress.

Morning sun sparkles on Summer's
burbles over worn smooth stones.

And to top it off—

Its banks are lush, covered with
Walt Whitman's sweet ground ivy.

> This is just to say,
> please let me know
> if you hear of a creek for sale,
> and I will give you
> a lifelong pass to wade in it,
> at any o'clock any day or night.

FLOWERED SUNDRESS ON CLOTHESLINE

Hoverflies are crucial pollinators. They also fight against
aphids, thrips, scale insects, and leaf-eating caterpillars.

for Kelle Green

Hoverflies
tiniest bee-lookalikes
glossy
darting swiping
>seduced by swaying
>turquoise jonquils
>purple apple blossoms

buzzing softly:
What rude magic is this?
No nectar, no pollen?
We've been exiled from
the way of flowers
>—*we must right this.*

REGARDING CERTAIN WILDFLOWERS

When arranging blossoms
in a shallow bowl
    woad
    black-eyed susan
    sweet woodruff
do take care
to wear gloves

else the blue dye of the woad leaf
combined with the golden essence
of the snappy black-eyed susan
will produce green stains on your lily whites
the likes of which
you have never before tried to get off.

The shy white woodruff
is of course innocent,
guilty of nothing more than
wafting the sweet scent of hay.

A WAY OF SEEING

Krista Kelley Walsh Installation 2010

A valley's sedate landscape
is turned upside down
when you see it through
a sunlit, water-filled vase.
Magical
how treetops become
roots, nourished
by underwater clouds.

After a desert rain
a tadpole, nurtured
by water as scant as
a cirrus strand,
morphs into a spade-foot toad
in less than two weeks.

A WONDER

Jacquie Trudeau

Her spirit
how it melds
in to everyone who loves her
makes them laugh and dance
when they didn't know
they wanted to.

Don't you ponder
how she does it?

And all the while she's
making decadent pies
or regaling us with stories
of questionable moral.

But it's her wisdom, isn't it?
How she shifts our view.
How she calms our crazy minds.

PERFECT SPACE

Patrick Scully

Am picturing
men's suit jackets, old & faded—
the ones I wore with
striped or polka-dot tights
when performing funky poetry
at Patrick's Cabaret
—and the others,
five in all each night who had
our fifteen minutes
in front of packed bleachers:
The safest stage on earth for
trembling emerging artists to
miraculously unfold petals
from bud to red-hot blossom
— 'e 'ad a vision 'ad us's Patrick
   an' ten-yeaar eftor ten-yeaar
   ta 30-yeaar na dayd 'e bahlk
Our own personal four-leaf clover.
Our own personal Saint Patrick.

SEIZE THE SUMMER

Scratch your athlete's foot
on the cool sinewy cord
of your hammock.

Grow giant watermelons
using droppings from
the Bat Goddess of Guano.

Prance round and round
in the lawn sprinkler
singing Figaro! Figaro!

And never never never
tell your mother-in-law
how to prune her roses.

NIGHT IN THE CITY

no
sirens

lush overgrown sumac
canopies the sidewalk
rustles

across the street
a Somali woman
draped in ochre
floats up the steps

a horn honks
car door
slams
mother-fuckin' tetrameter rap
roars by

leaning against the rickety
splintered porch rail
I see
one star
no
two

UGANDA

Midday. Sweltry.
Majestic languid lion
high in the umbrella fig tree
outstretched along a limb.
No tsetse flies up there.
No cattlemen, no poisoned fare.
A breath of air.

There is this about trees:
Sanctuary is their destiny.
Lions chameleons toucans agree.

AT THE BIRDFEEDER

Most colorful birds are male because
they're dispensable. Females are camou-
flaged so as to carry on the species.

The Red-Bellied Woodpecker
doesn't have a red belly

Finches, chickadees, grosbeaks,
even the boisterous blue jay—
all give way to him, all
intimidated by this painfully shy,
smartly handsome
Red-Bellied Woodpecker

dapper stripes with ivory vest
brilliantine red head

I know a woman whose flaming red hair
enters the room before she does:
Her blue serge suit and silk cream blouse
are so classy
women in silver lamé twinge with regret
even as they are drawn to her

her lilting voice
her fresh soap scent

LABYRINTH

Mossy paths lead
to center's stone bench
worn smooth by sojourners

You have wandered
to this verdant haven
like a bee drawn to
bluebells in springtime

Maybe you will have
a vision
as you sit in reverie

Maybe not

It's possible to
simply pluck the minutes
soaked in sunshine
until you rise
buoyant

STRAW MULES

Bought because mules are good for
shuffling around the house, handmade
with sea-green silk flowers across the toe.

The flaxen straw with its muslin lining
crunched and talked to her, coaxed her to
plan a trip to St. Maarten, told her not to miss
the underwater fireflies in Oyster Bay
on a moonless night.

Her mother says only lazy shiftless people shuffle.

Or, a trip to St. Thomas where there's a slim
chance of spying iridescent turquoise on
black wings: Shimmery Jamaica Kite butterfly
—poached and pinned almost to extinction
    but never ever daunted.

A REAL PEACH

natural
platinum
blonde
beautiful
irresistible
soft white
downy
facial hair
lickable
not a bit
like
icky
peach fuzz
–just goes
to show
you gotta
peel
your peach

LUST-CUM-LEMON

Rocked against a hard surface
to loosen opaque nectar

Magic liqueur oozes
through practiced fingers,
its cool tangy kiss
performs miracles—

> the limp oyster perks,
> a mound of black caviar
> turns to milky gray ambrosia
>
> even sugar puckers
> in piquant lemon marmalade
> more lickable
> than lapped cream

PALS

For Maudie

At midnight I accost you and
know you positively understand
what I mean when I say
Happy New Year, dear friend,
Happy Glorious New Year, and
many more adventures for us—

We'll nod to wild buttercups & daisies
during our treks to
find sweet ripe mulberries
and water cress
while we listen to the *coo-OH-oo*
of doves flirting in the cedar trees

BEAUTY

Some
times
beauty
is so
STARTLING
it snaps me in two
and half of me
      gasps
while the other half
      whispers
kneel
kneel down before it

WE HAVE SEEN THE GREATER GODDESS
AND SHE LOOKS JUST LIKE US

Her scent is salt
and honey and
ocean and blood

In the evening
she slowly licks
her full ready lips,
dark eyes flashing

At daybreak
she leaves, laughing
as everyman lunges
to grab her ankles
    she will not stay
    for anything he has

Her bare feet
trail powdery prints
like the beat of
the luna moth's wings

and wild beasts
do not confuse her

CIRCADIAN RHYTHM

Try to snuggle me first thing in the morning
and I'll screech like a banshee and
set my catahoula hound to howling

But — come midday
when the fish don't bite
and the birds go silent

in that sultry quiet

my hormones start beating a tom-tom

        heat shimmers
        pressure rises

until my pheromone perfume commands
my subjects to bow down and into my thighs

as though I were
Aphrodite

and I certainly am
The Goddess
transformed

PARTNERSHIP

Venus
raw earthy
goddess of ripe impulse

takes pity on your plight
loosens the rein
on your teenage
whorl of passion

and there you go frisky free
coupling in your boudoir
—until a sound disrupts:

melodic chirrups
of the Lark, on guard
at the House of Capulet

WE

Bill Panger

Center to center
in our lazy afternoon bed
we hear Cardinal's
cheer cheer cheer.

I nip crunchy chocolate
from off a Nut Goodie bar,
pass the sweetness
from my mouth to yours.

My fingers map
your tan rugged face
over and over,
earmark it mine, mine.

EAU DE TOILETTE

A stud.
Rugged.
Handsome.
Sensitive.
Caring.
Strong enough
to lift his consort.
Smells good, wears
Gucci Guilty *pour homme* perfume,
not Gucci Guilty *pour homme* cologne.
Can afford
Gucci Guilty *pour homme* perfume.
Buys his consort
Gucci shoes and bags and evening gowns.
Works for Gucci.
Gets a discount.

LET ME MAKE YOU MINE

Oh Jacquie, Wendy, Bill, Al,
let me be your sycophant.

I will praise you to the skies,
fulfill your every wish,
fawn all over you.
Your beslobbered,
back-scratching disciple.
Your servile parasite.

Oh Jacquie, Wendy, Bill, Al,
let me be your ultimate flatterer.

Let me be anything you want,
just please don't let me be.

GARAGES

In Lake Havasu City, a man has
a marble garage floor—shiny black
with silver flecks, accented by
shiny red and yellow baseboards.

In a garage in Minnesota hangs
a Tiffany chandelier, "Moose at Dusk"
to light up perfectly the hunter's Hummer
and the wife's Softail Harley-Davidson.

I had a bootlegger uncle in Oklahoma
who hid his bullet-ridden Terraplane Coupe
in a ramshackle shed, so Ness's T-men
wouldn't know he was richer than God.

If you think I'm saying it takes all kinds,
well, I swear on
my rattling Dodge Ram,
it does.

CONSIDER INSANITY

That there be no more madness,
let there be many more quips about

the blonde who was so dumb
he mistook a woman for an object.

That there be no more madness,
let there be many more rubdowns:

warm lavender oil massaged
deep into woman's fed-up bones.

That there be no more madness,
hie thee to that lair of laughter

where the joke's on
anyone caught proprietary.

COCKSCOMB vs. COXCOMB

At the ranch
a rooster aims a hose
watering flowers lining
the chicken yard fence.

Hens and chicks
peck peck corn,
the affable rooster careful
not to get them wet.

He's kind, unlike the crazy
fool coxcomb foreman.

ECLIPSE

Opposites
attract.

Hot-plasma sun
and
delicate-air moon
seldom kiss—
although
when they do,
they kiss
in the dark
and millions
of us
know
what's up.

SANS A LOVER

She looked at the chocolate malt
just made in her new malt machine
and the strawberry malt next to it—

calculated them to be two portions
of creamy makeshift sex.

A bicycle tire goes flat
when the bike isn't ridden for
a long period of time—clearly,
the pressure differential
between inside and outside
causes air to leak from the valve stem
requiring the tire to be pumped up.

CONSTANT CARPING

It doesn't matter
who takes out the garbage,

but if it does,
something is muchly wrong
and must needs be fixed.

Like the drip drip of a faucet
it will drive you mad
and who needs that?

Perhaps you need counselling
or a divorce lawyer
or a sojourn to the sea,

or maybe, just maybe
you simply need to find
your sense of humor.

SALT

In Leonardo da Vinci's The Last Supper, *Judas,
who is sitting next to Jesus, has spilled the salt.*

Spilling the salt is not like
spilling the beans—little bombs
pelting someone's surprise party.
Spilled salt asks better of us,
wants to be thrown over the left
shoulder to avoid future mishaps,
wants us to leave nothing to chance
no matter how remote.
What have we got to lose?

SIX DOWN, ONE TO GO

Behind the seventh veil
a belly jiggles
breasts sway.

The king's tongue lolls out
like a hungry dog
drooling for its dinner.

The veil drops.

The king drops
from cardiac arrest,
speechless ever after.

Some stories
definitely need to have
a different ending.

$E = mc^2$

If I could get my reluctant body
up to a speed of
   thirty-four billion
   seven hundred million
   nine hundred eighty-three thousand
   five hundred and twenty-four
miles per second

I'd disappear

or rather
at deadly velocity
I'd turn into invisible energy

so much energy, Albert,
I wouldn't know
what to do with myself.

MENOPAUSE WHORL

The snakebird
sinks slowly into water
until only the tip of her bill
can be seen—then
plunges
snatches her target fish
swims to the surface
flips her prey into the air
and
swallows it head first.

ANOTHER BLOODY HYSTERECTOMY POEM

Good-bye.
Good riddance.
Relieved. Restored. With no
loss of menstrual powers that
linked me to the moon—
      If I want,
      I can capture
      the handsome young
      man
      or woman
      under lunar light.
Perhaps you've noticed
I haven't
spewed on, hissed at, or choked
a single soul
since the doctor threw the whole wad
over her shoulder.

QUEENS AND EX-KINGS

The Queen of Hearts
trapped between King with his sword
and mustachioed Jack with his ax

escaped with the other three Queens
—four of a kind
who dealt their own winning hand.

In full regalia, mounted on mares,
their quartet galloped hither and yon

rescuing all trapped Queens,
routing all Kings and Jacks.

Yes, they took over the Roundtable.
Yes, they effected an equitable Queendom.

Grand Slam.

MUCHNESS

There are certain women who
aren't scattered when shattered,
custom-made solids
with extraordinary atomic structure,
able to pick themselves up in one piece
only to ride the winds again & again.
You needn't bother,
you'll never catch one.

PRETTY VISAGE

Sitting at a sidewalk café,
a lady of the demimonde,
creamy long legs crossed
martini in one hand
ebony cigarette-holder in the other.

—Startled
she laughs at the cloudburst,
turns up her face to the sky
to feel the rainy comedy act.

OPENING NIGHT FOR
AVERY HOPWOOD'S
GARDEN OF EDEN, 1927

All the way from Alabama to London's
grand Lyric Theatre—
Tallulah Bankhead center stage,
beautiful, vivacious
(oh, that sexy throaty voice)
inciting cheers and gasps
scandalous
tossing the corset and blazing forth
in silk *crêpe de chine* undies!

Bewitched by Tallulah's
outrageous antics, a bona fide
Tallulah Gallery Girl
checks her 'Victory Red' lipstick,
the only shade Tallulah ever wore.

If only to have been there . . .

SISYPHIA'S SOLUTION
after Krista Kelley Walsh installation

Muscles stretched
deep breath taken
she grasps the sledgehammer

    heaves smashes pulverizes

ignoring hundreds of stone chips
flying off the end of every arc

In labored time she finishes,
dusts off her hands

    saunters to the top of her mound

The rest of us are compelled
to rush to the hardware store,
fired up, inspired by

    her grasp of the hickory handle

ADVICE

The talented Cherokee boy can't read is sixteen in seventh
grade is flunking every class is even flunking art, has sent
his art teacher crying from the room after he picked up the
paintbrush and slathered black all over his shiny silvery
walleye, created scale by scale over three weeks—the fish
he has filleted into crispy fried trips to the principal's office
and served to himself on a platter etched with shoulds.

Yet, when his grandmother tells him he'd as well forget
about school—*Go live by the lake, paint everything the
great mystery has put there from the reeds to the sun and
sell it to the white man at inflated prices*—the boy grins,
shrugs, enrolls for Driver's Ed.

NATIVE AMERICAN GROUPIE

Surely no one
can blame
a white woman
for going to a pow-wow,
lured
from her therapist
by the silver tinkling cones of a
'Healing Jingle Dress Dance'
—a sky-blue jingle dress
    a sun-yellow jingle dress
    an apricot-moon jingle dress
    a star-white jingle dress

WOMAN SENSE

for Treasa Rae Willis

Don't come crawling back to me.
Don't you dare call me 'Honey'
all teary-eyed
wanting forgiveness
whining about
how blissful we were.
Just get out of here, go back to
your other countless coy prey.

I gave you all the love I had, Casanova.
Don't come to Mama now, Baby, uh-uh.

SOUFFLÉ

deflated
withered
a mere shadow
of its potential
letting her down as it went down
when all she wanted
was to impress the person
she most wanted
to impress—
     a soufflé's behest
     bidding her not to put all her
     egg whites in one basket

TRUST

When a certain one
again betrays our trust,
it's easy to give up on them,
the old *do-it-to-me-once* thing.

A hard wrestle it is
to trust again.

When frayed rope
dangles the tire swing,
to swing or not to swing
as though we have a choice.

THE MAKING OF A SCREW

You take a piece of birch in one hand,
then twist it past a knife grasped in
the other, the blade angled to the shaft,
the knife scribing a spiral on the wood.

You do this over and over
until you have a pile of screws
and a pile of shavings.

You use the screws to build
a rock-a-bye cradle, and use
the shavings to stuff the pillow
for the wee babe's head.

Cradle and all
Mommy will catch baby
when the bough breaks.

THE LITTLE ONES

When a running toddler
falls so hard
she needs stitches in her knee
it's because she can't take her eyes
off the hopping bunny
the fluttery orange monarch.

And when a two-year-old
says again and again
No! and Mine!
it's because he knows
his cherub face can cast a spell on
even the mighty oak, make it sway.

We must eagerly with aforethought
seek out these girls and boys,
get them to tell us their secrets,
bribe them—
sweets in exchange for
innocent wonderment
and chin-up confidence.

A LEARNING

On a sunny morning exploration
a child found an angel made of
heavy binding twine wrapped
round and round a cone—
      the angel's wings, fragile parchment
      its head, a wimpled apple
a head without mouth or nose or eyes
but of such sweet aura
the child ever after
thought all angels to be faceless.

HOME

One dented metal chair
painted over the years white, red, black
intercepts light
from one open window.

On faded cracked linoleum
in the chair's cone shadow
a child is on her knees playing jacks.

I never was good at it.

MAGGIE'S GIFT

Maggie 'Blu' Kjeer

A single dandelion in its own
miniature crystal vase—
chosen with care, picked with love:
tiny, tiny rays of sunshine.

I once knew a dandelion personally and
envied the way she bent with the breeze.

I do so hope you have
a darling neighbor with
sparkling eyes, skipping
bearing gifts of crystal and earth.

LET THE SKY BE THE LIMIT

Skinned knees primly crossed,
ruffled dress spotted with ketchup,
she coos and sings, bent
over the rag doll in her lap.

But now she hears something,
lifts her head—
might be the wind in the tire swing
might be the ice cream cart.

She's gone, the dropped-doll
lies contorted on the grass
near the tossed magic wand.

Wherever she is
let her be.

Let her build a spaceship
and pilot it fearless.

Let her rattle the cage
of everyone on Mars.

THE FIVE-YEAR-OLD AND
THE CABLE REPAIRMAN

Knowing who it is, she sends
her grandson to the door and
stops dead when she hears him
parrot his grandfather:
*Are you the stupid s.o.b. who
took off the boofercate and
hooked the cable to the living room
where there isn't even a TV?*

She watches the big man's smile
collapse into a rueful sigh:
Yep, that's me all right.

She grins as the child thrusts out
his arm for a handshake, the way
his grandfather taught him:
*You want a coke or coffee or
a Girl Scout cookie?*

OYEZ! OYEZ! OYEZ!

At a formica kitchen table patterned
with pink and grey boomerangs,
a 7-year-old and her 6-year-old brother
play five-card-draw with toothpick-antes.

*You're cheating! You only get to
draw four cards if you have an ace!*

I HAVE AN ACE! I DON'T CHEAT!

ALICE IN CONUNDRUMLAND

At the Mall of America
she has not once
sidestepped a bicycler
nor has a single bunny
hopped across her path.

Oh dear! Oh dear! said Alice,
Where is the golden key
to Garden's bright flowers
and cool fountains?

6, 28, 496, 8128

Old MacDonald had a farm
and on that farm he had
six perfect cows
before he sold one
to the Farmer in the Dell
whose nurse's cow had died.

Certified mathematicians one
and all are in agreement that
'perfect numbers' are fun, but
of no use in our imperfect world.

After all, who among us is not
the sum of all our factors?
One farmer + five cows = Perfect.

EEE-I-EEE-I-OOH!

TATTLETALE

One time
a bad guy did a good
and a good guy
did a bad.
Someone saw the good guy
do the bad.
And told.
Someone saw the bad guy
do the good.
And never said a word.

The time to run tell Mom is
when your sister's cut is gushing—
or when
a bad guy does a good.

ACCOUNTING COURSE 101

Back then we traded comics—
Archie was worth two Felix the Cat, and
Wonder Woman worth a Popeye, a Caspar,
and a Dale Evans Queen of the West.
Dick Tracy, the most valuable of all, could
cost as much as six of any of the others.

Trading comics was a life lesson:
You get what you pay for.

GOODY TWO-SHOES

Saved my pennies in a piggy bank
cleaned my plate
curtsied and said please
never cheated at hopscotch
nor sassed my mother
nor kissed my cousins in secret.

How I envied
the girl next door
who drove adults to distraction—
smacked her gum in public and
never wore socks with her oxfords.

All of us on the block
liked her best.

THESIS

The square root of an orange
is one orange—
1 orange x 1 orange = 1 orange.
The same is true
of an ocean wave.

Your essay question is:
Which is more fun—
to play in the dip and rise
of an ocean wave or
to squirt your sister in the eye
with your orange's juice?

Include the *why?* and *how?*
and the *why not?* and *how not?*
to prove your choice
is the only possible choice
relative to square roots.

TEEN UPHEAVAL

Her hormones
pick her up
slam her against the wall
pick her up
slam her against the wall
pick her up . . .
until she folds
into fetal retreat,
but even then, they whisper
     you're ugly
     you're nobody
and there is nothing
a mother can do.

YESTERDAY DAYDREAM

Sheer organdy curtains
at the open window
swirl and sway with the breeze
in sync with jiving radio jazz,
pushing the teenager forward
to risqué nights,
carrying her out of captivity
into high-heels & fringed scarlet
dancing scandalous
at the Cotton Club—

And she hasn't a clue that lying
across the bed by the window,
imagining it,
is as good as it gets.

SHURI

Sixteen years old.
Fashion plate nonpareil:
  split-toe black knee high boots
  blue basket-weave rib socks
  frayed piqué wrap-skirt, iron buckle
  silver twined bracelets on each upper arm
  polished iron breastplate and bevor
  hair black corn-row braids
  beautiful white-dotted African face
Black Panther vambraces shoot azure blue high IQ.

CUT IT!
CUT!
CUT!
CUT!

Mom.
Teaching me how to
parallel park.
You don't know what
hysterical laughter is
until a day out with Mom
on a you-can-do-it
stick-shift excursion
prepping me for my
Driver's License exam.

HANGING OUT WITH DAD

Mom had a hissy fit when
I accidentally poured bleach
instead of soap
onto the washer load—
It ruined the hot pink blouse
she was going to wear on a date
with her new boyfriend Mike.
Dad grinned when I told him.
He said he
never did like that blouse.

HEALING RITUALS

Time and again
Mom rubbed my growing pains
slowly kneading witch hazel
into every cramped calf muscle,

and then I'd rub her feet
swollen and red
from nine hours rushing table
to table and back at the café.

A few of us—
aunt cousin grandma me mom
at last light
sat on the porch,
brushed one another's hair with
natural bristles from Fuller Brush.

SACROSANCT

for Damon

Silence
    not *stony*
    not *awkward*
    not *icy*
    not *heavy*
Space
where space
did not
exist

AD INFINITUM

When a pair of the world's lovers
split up
because one or the other abandons the other

a *she* keens
a *he* caves up
for there is no pain as cruel as abandonment.

Yet, by and by time assuages.
Repeat.
Repeat.

A red-winged blackbird
will slam into a plate-glass window
time and again.

No hindsight.
No foresight.
Not an inkling.

ON BALANCE

Didn't do the laundry.
Didn't vacuum.
Didn't pick up clutter.

Took Cousin Lilah
who never smiles
for a walk three
times this week.

She almost smiled—once,
when a tiny green frog
jumped onto her foot.

ELDER LADY IN TWILIGHT BLUE HOUR

No mud pies.
No chasing toads in scuffed sandals.
No race to the ice cream cart's bell.
No Mama at bedtime *Sleep tight, I love you.*

In long indigo shadows
laughter and weeping
play musical chairs.

FAMILY REUNION

On benches next to the playground
mottled leathery hands ward off water
gun attacks by freckled little leaguers
and affectionately pat little tushies
toddling by à la Charlie Chaplin.

Most of the teenagers stayed home.

Clustered in schlepped lawn chairs
mothers sip iced tea, muse over who
probably won't be here next year
and who's having the next baby.

Who made this peach cobbler? I have to
get this recipe, does anyone know who
made this scrumptious peach cobbler?
The crust just melts in your mouth.

DAUGHTER DAMON MOVING
TO CALIFORNIA AT AGE 18

You are as lithe
and beautiful
as a puma

and granted
just as swift and clever,
yet even so, be careful.

Tawny cats
lazing in the sun
eyes half-closed

often do not see the flicker—

sun's glint on steel
a split second
before the shot is fired.

IMPERATIVE

for Mike 'Hoss' Clyburn

Civvies
must be hand-tailored
flawless
couture designed to conceal
prostheses and braces.

A tortoise without its shell
is subjected to pity—an insult to
the dignity of a survivor paragon.

Myriad soldiers carry
the weight of battle
inside their broken bodies—
We damn well better salute them.

NO WARNING

Lightning
jagged white electroshock
space split apart
wind vicious vicious
torrents pounding
splintering everything.

Shaken
but not bent
she survived the cancer
quieted herself
slept.

Next morning
when she re-entered the world
the air smelled like a meadowlark:

She heard his clear flute song
before she saw his classy yellow vest.

He saw her too, and sang her name.

NATURAL SELECTION

In her room
were many houses and a boat.

Every year the room got
smaller and smaller as the houses
and the boat got bigger and bigger
—until the room could no longer contain
the houses and the boat, such that
it had to burst and crush her.

As she lay healing in the hospital
surrounded by *hybrid tea roses*
and *tinted carnations,*
she realized what she really wanted—
a huge old-fashioned snapdragon
a snapdragon so big she could crawl
inside its golden mouth and sing there
and rock the potbellied baby
with the flies on its face.

NOON MEAL

Between bites of fried chicken
and mashed potatoes and gravy,
the hired hands laughed about
what they'd do to any damn fag
who ever set foot on *this* farm.

Sweltering by the hot stove,
Ma brushed a fly from her
sweating glass of lemonade,
took a long swig, slowly exhaled,
thinking of what Pa used to say:

You can't teach a pig to change,
just wastes your time and
irritates the hell out of the bigot.

IF

If the natives
had not been slaughtered
or caged
they would have fared well,
for they did not
pierce a salmon in spawn
nor harvest wild rice
before it was ripe.

Smaller and smaller
schools of salmon
struggle upstream in
cold numb silence, and many
wash up on shore, dead.

The Hitchiti
took care of the stream.
The Anadarko
took care of the honey bees.
These are the ones we need.

GRANARY

Spontaneous combustion
ignites the grain,
consumes it in a roaring inferno—
impervious to tamping or banking,
like the wildfires ignited by
politicians and oil barons.

There's no stopping it,
no way to clean up afterward:
Ashes slick.
Ashes stuck to every single thing.
Indelible.

MACRO

AIRBORNE SEX à la BUTTERFLIES

swooooosh—bump

swooooosh—bump

bump swoosh

bump flut
bump flut
bump flut

flut bump
　swoosh bump
　　flut bump

flut-flut-flut
bump-bump-bump-bump-bump
bump-bump-bump-bump-bump
flut-bump
flut
bump

aahhhhh

　　　flit

　　　　　flut

　　　　　　　flop

twitter

AN OLD CUSTOM

The first year of marriage, put a bean in a jar
every time you make love, then take a bean out
each time in the years thereafter. Ancient Greece

Unnoticed by the newlyweds
sun bounced off
the blue glass canning jar
ready on the bedside table.

Neither of them thought about beans
not planting
not watching them grow
not the harvest.

Later, much later the same day
he stood and dropped five pintos
into the glass jar as she
grinned and watched, clapping.

The first year
the space between beans and lid
decreased dramatically.

The second year
sometimes she or he
remembered to remove a few.

Of their five remarkable daughters
one kept the dusty blue jar
half full of beans,
planted pintos in her garden
come spring.

STAGGERS AND SPAVINS

Like a horse with a hitch
in its get-along,
she wobbled and winced her way
up the museum steps.

She hadn't known she
would see Picasso's *Rocinante*,
would laugh herself to tears.

Pablo Picasso 1955   Authorized *Fair Use*

GREAT-GRANDMOTHER

◊

Recollecting during afternoon tea,
she announced it's the *whales* who
are grateful to Caresse Crosby:
>*Two handkerchiefs*
>*and a bit of pink ribbon*
>*usurped the corset*
>*and made our lives heaven.*

◊

She said to me one full-moon night:
>*It isn't the ambient light*
>*that's keeping you awake,*
>*it's the sugar you ate—*
>*you should have eaten meat,*
>*meat knocks you dead on your feet.*

◊

At the glam gala garden party
she held out her prize for all to see,
as proud as she used to be when
she baked a devil's food cake—

Neither you nor I can know the glee
of catching a toad at age ninety-three.

GRAVITY

aah
yes
eyelids
breasts
belly
P
U
L
L
E
D
toward
the
center
of
the
earth
eventually
slipping
down
and
off
like
the
discarded
peel
of
a
scalded
tomato
ready
for
canning
leaving
only
juicy
pulp

NAKED

damp
puckered
sliding on the wet tile floor
after a summer bath

I face the full mirror and
admire your reflection
my body

your age spots
      on opalescent crepe skin
your clumsy geometry
      sagging concave curves
      isosceles grey patch molting

sunlight and shadow
accent your perfect
imperfections

      scars
      from wars won and lost against
      aphids, apathy, city hall

      keepsakes
      from hot buttered biscuits
      and wild nights rollicking

arms curved above my head
I dance sway twirl

      intoxicated
      by a sweet lilting melody—
      flutes and laughter of tomorrow

I can't help myself
I adore you

EVERY EARLY JUNE

A ninety-year-old woman climbs
her backyard pear tree
gingerly
careful not to damage the limbs,
for the tree is older than she—

> arms abreast the trunk
> left foot first on to a burl
> cross right foot over to
> branch, left foot following
> repeat with next burl, then
> wriggle butt on to larger branch
> dangle legs

Thus stationed,
she hums *A Good Man Is Hard to Find*
as she surveys her strawberry patch:
berries almost red-ripe for picking,
planted not long after she wed the
handsome man
who turned into Mr. Hyde.

Her deeply lined mouth
twitches into a grin, quickly
overtaken by cackles and
cackles and cackles and cackles,
clearly heard by all the neighbors.

She can't control herself
at the thought of her husband
buried under that strawberry patch,
a butcher knife in his chest—
no doubt rusted by now.

What? You want to know
how a wizened old lady
can climb a huge old pear tree?
Just think about it . . .
She lived happily ever after.

ECOSYSTEM

◊

Cherished are the neighbors
who rescue locked-out teens
and stroll with dogs abandoned
for the sake of a vacation:

the Thompsons trim
the Holmquists' hedge
the Holmquists bring in
the Goldsteins' mail
the Goldsteins fill
the Browns' birdbath
the Browns bake apple pie
    for Widow Fushikoshi.

I myself am inclined to
call the Pound the next time
Mrs. Thompson's poodle
scats on my petunias.

◊

On a warm pleasant evening
we neighbors gather one and all
in Widow Fushikoshi's backyard
to celebrate her daughter's wedding
and savor the luxury of homemade
daifuku sweet rice cakes.

We laugh softly and chat
as dulcet melodies of the koto
mingle with the honey fragrance of
Japanese jasmine—starlight clusters
on succulent vines, entwined.

◊

Mrs. Thompson gave me
the pick of the litter.
The Pound? Not an option.

MY LOVER'S WILD LIFE

Bill Panger

Across crunchy snow
every morning
you schlep corn for the deer,
suet for downy woodpeckers.

With coffee and a cigarette you squint
over the Times crossword, then
take off for work—slamming the brakes
to pick up fresh roadkill for a trophy tail.

And every day you create:
choosing wood over pergo,
your deft fingers crafting perfect
spaces in imperfect houses.

After a humongous dinner
it's football time, when you
fall asleep in your recliner
with two little dogs on board.

On crunchy snow
every morning
corn for deer
suet for woodpeckers.

Nothing exciting until week's end:
poker with the guys,
athletic games with me
on a field of green-striped sheets.

MADAME TUSSAUD

Farmer Furlong,
nicknamed *No-Nonsense*
by neighbor farmers,
did not believe in
UFOs
or an afterlife
or the power of
dimwitted water dowsers.

On a particular day
Farmer Furlong
had reason to pause
to watch
an intrepid field mouse.
A field mouse with its
back bent
breathing hard
sweaty
under the weight
of a hillock
hoisted on its shoulders.

In a daze
Farmer Furlong
followed the mouse
to the northeast corner
of the back forty
where it eased
the hillock down,
squeaking a bit
at the effort.

Farmer Furlong
stood still
riveted
while
his face to his ankles
turned as pale as
a waxwork.
Yes, did Farmer Furlong
transfigure.

IMP'S REWARD

I once saw a sapajou monkey
sitting on a hand organ
scratching her head
wondering what to do
while the grinder napped,

until recklessly, swiftly, she grabbed her
tin cup, scaled the brick wall above the
grinder's head and dangled from
a ledge two stories up—squealing,
chattering, waving the cup in delight—
center stage.

Not a bad trick in Manhattan, to command
the attention of frenzied rushing hordes.

Laughing in admiration,
I couldn't help wondering
where she got the cigar band
sported on her opposable thumb;
was it carelessly dropped by
a puffing corporate honcho?

More likely the paper ring was a gift
from the alluring street walker
who carefully clipped the end of her
imported Macanundo before she lit up.

MANUAL ELEVATOR

The elevator operator had a raspy voice
like Thelma Ritter and Selma Diamond,
and a smile just as wide and welcome—
especially when
her white-gloved hand
tweaked the cheek of a child
(whose own children would never see
a suited-up elevator operator)

She let the children try to turn
the heavy bronze crank-handle
that hoisted them to:

> "Mezzanine! Housewares! Restrooms!
> Watch your step!"

Miss Thelma Selma had no smile
for buxom ladies in Catalina knit suits
who farted on board
then looked askance
as though someone else had done it

ICON ACTOR

Long after his death
Rudolph Valentino's
magnetism
prompted men everywhere
to learn the tango
and learn
how to pop their eyes
and bare their teeth
while making love.

Popped eyes?
Bared teeth?
Makes you wonder
what all those
hordes of women fans
saw in him,
what the mystery woman
veiled in black
was thinking
when she placed
a single red rose
on his grave
every year,
year after year.

1970's PREFERRED STOCKS

The three-year-old ate
stock certificates for lunch.
The first time she requested them
instead of peanut butter and jelly,
her father was dismayed.
He tried to persuade her to eat
the Daily Market Analysis or
Stock Value Tables, but to no avail.

In desperation her father explained
that stock certificates are like money
and if she continued to eat them
her college fund would end up
in the sewer system—
to which she nodded wide-eyed as
she stuffed IBM into her fat little cheeks.

She grew up to be a stockbroker.
Whenever she encountered a client
who took credit himself for his gains
but blamed her for his losses,
his new stock certificates
would mysteriously disappear—
and when she burped after lunch,
CUSIP numbers floated in the air.

FOOD & DRINK

It's ironic how
some of us want to fly to Paris
and drink chicory coffee
at a sidewalk café while
we devour beignets
or
want to be oared down the Nile
like Cleopatra,
eating succulent grapes
and pine nuts
fed to us by a tawny entourage
or
want to bask in the pleasure
of drinking finest vodka
with Russian poets.

All this we crave, and more.

But then comes old age and
we're bored with the whole lot—
nothing satiates
except meatloaf and
mashed potatoes and
scratch chocolate cake with
cooked white frosting,
and later, under the moon
an iced tea
with a twist of pity
for Cleopatra.

ON A SEASHORE
Variations on a theme from Tom Waits

She loves herself
and I guess she always will
ever since she put her picture in a frame,
and what she really, really wants
is to dance real slow with her man.

So she's gone and shed her shoes
for a stroll along the beach, searching
through the noisy Sunday crowd,
yes she's gone and shed those shoes
on a quest for her two-timing man.

Now she's gone and shed her clothes
Monday morning on the beach, when
there isn't any noise or a crowd,
yes, she's gone and gotten naked—
never mind a devil two-timing man.

She loves herself
and I guess she always will
ever since she put her picture in a frame,
but what she really, really wants
is a drop-dead stunner bronze tan.

EVENING FALLS

Le Soir qui tombe 1964, René Magritte

At sundown
with lust aforethought
you burst through her window
laughing softly
and for hours make her
shiver and moan
because you want to
(so much so, you've shattered
a perfectly good window)
and all the while you whisper and
murmur that she us creamy, flawless.

Long before the shards of glass
take on dawn's glow
she shimmies and picks up the beat—
a get-down-and-boogie goddess
who's realized
there wasn't a thing wrong
with her big, big hips
that a broken window couldn't fix.

CINDERELLA:
ALL THOSE YEARS OF WASTED VIRTUE

I continued devout and good precisely as dictated by those Grimm men. Fifty dragged-out years did I light the fires and haul water for black hearts, before finally making it to the ball after praying on my mother's grave.

At last there we were, the prince and I, at the center of a magnificent ballroom (marble floor, grand chandelier), spot-lighted in a rumba: stomachs in, backs straight. I let him lead.

We danced as one, his red satin tuxedo pressed against my skintight red satin dress. (His mother insisted on matching outfits.) Our hips swayed in sultry sync, our steps entwined in seamless motion, undulating to the slow-quick-quick beat of the African drum.

But this was not as easy as it sounds: Step right, left, right, brush right, move forward turning half-left to back into the prince's right arm into sweetheart position—at which point the prince, overwhelmed by desire, grasped me, clutched me to his pec's. I was so overcome I swooned, and chirred, like an alarm clock . . .

Alarm clock?
A long night's dream?

No matter—we would have lived with his mother. Besides, I'd rather daydream, about line dancing at the rodeo, with the promise of a sweaty buckin' honcho between my legs.

Breasts heaving, nostrils flared, cinders sticky.

DRUMBEATS

In the spirit of Al Perkins 1904-1975

Mind mind, numb numb
do-nothing doing nothing
hum ho hum
mind on hold, mind in hole
do-nothing, do-nothing
can't go go

Rev up mind, stop ho hum
do something, do something
thrum thrum thrum

Trim that bower
fix that shower
clear a path
dog needs a bath
house needs a coat
fix leaky boat

do something
do something
run rush run

Mind, mind
numb, numb
steady
that
hammock
cause
here
I come

drum roll
drum roll
drum
drum
drum

MR. EGO

Spurned? Me?

Roaring inferno
        ravager
        of moist dew-covered coffers
        devourer
        of cradled soft petals

Blazing fury
        stunned by cold water
        choking on flying ash
        amazed
        that any brazen splash would dare
        rebut
        his superb phallus aflame

Quenched
        by a cascade
        of cold shoulder

Quivers
        into damp
        snuffed
        embers

I TOOK MY RED HEART OUT OF HIS
PURPLE PASSION AND LEFT HIM BLUE

Mom warned me to stay away from
people who pull you down,
which is why I gave *Himself* the boot—
I got tired of him thinking he owned
what is rightfully mine:

These breasts glistening with apricot oil,
this heart tattoo on my butt—
even my toenails (he had a foot fetish)
painted bright red
because Aunt Melva's bright red toenails
always looked so pretty in her strap sandals.

I sure am sorry you never met Aunt Melva,

never saw her during harvest time
cooking ham hocks & beans for 15 hired hands
looking cool as a cucumber
in her hotter than hot kitchen
      rolled-up jeans
      long white man's shirt
never saw her bang out boogie-woogie piano
at the Farmer's Union meetings, enormous
silver rings jiving on her muscled fingers.

The next time I polish my toenails
I won't even think about Mr. Foot Fetish—
I'll just remember Aunt Melva
and all the other women I know
who oil their own breasts.

SWEET DREAM

For Dhyani Ywahoo, Etowah Band
Eastern Cherokee Tsalagi Nation

The child sleeps in her new moccasins,
loves the way the doe's soft skin
takes the shape of her feet

In midnight's dream
she stirs
hears drums
hears the heart chant
echoing compassion

> ah ni ko ko nay
> > ah ni ko nay
> > > tesh na ha ha

She sees three fires

> > > red
> > yellow
> blue

Prettier than anything can be

Out of these three sacred fires
all other colors shoot like roman candles
> orange orioles
> > lime caterpillars
> > > johnny-purple-jump-ups

When the child tiptoes
tranced
closer and closer to the fires,
whirling embers
do not sting her

REVERIE

a
  rock
is
  fall
ing
    in
slow
    mo
tion
    down
the
    rus
ty
  clay
    walls
of
  Palo
Duro
  can
yon

Sweet thinking of him
lulls her to sleep,
shadows her through the day.
She wants him to rise from the grave,
wants them to sit again, rub knees
under the table they made
for their house on the canyon's rim.

the
  water-
worn
  rock
hits
  the canyon floor
bounces
  in umber dust

SNORKELING IN CARIBBEAN
AKUMAL, MEXICO

Bill Panger

and the sea
round about and over me
in my creases
caressing my curves
all around as blue as
a peacock's blue-green shimmer
and you my love
holding my hand
giving me courage gently in our slow slow swim

steering me around fragile coral
      antique lace
      touched scarred

      like my own scars
      left by the water moccasin
      one foot from my face
      as I dog-paddled in
      the murky river muddy red
            shiny scales arched neck glint eyes
            fanged cotton mouth
            poised to strike
      the near miss that scared me away
      from *all* waters

until you my love
brought me here
to a paradise of darting colors
our aqua playground
where reef fishes flirt
      spotlight parrot
      yellowtail damsel
and I beat my flippers
pull at your hand to go faster faster
and
then
you turn me loose
let me go
let me dash
after red purple orange fishes

AFTER A HARD DAY'S WORK

Big fingers
   sinewy
   from pulling teats
   and pushing the plow,
   peppered
   with scrubbed
   ground-in dirt,
pull the dainty thread
through the taut cloth.

A hoop is held close to his overall bib,
his white forehead over a red face
furrowed in concentration.

So engrossed is he in his
dishtowel embroidery—
lazy-daisy petal stitches,

he does not look up
when the TV announces
a rise in corn prices.

It is the habit of daisies
to close their petals
when the sun goes down.

Outside the window
white rays fold over
golden disks,

taking quiet notice
of a steady worker,
letting him be.

THROUGH BRAMBLE BUSHES

Hounds gain on fox.
Brittle twigs snap.

Every day
you meet yourself coming & going
racing across the
bridge to and from work
without so much as a blink at
the river passing under or
landscapes hurtling past
blurred by the crammed schedule
rushing through your head.

That fox
never once
looked back at the hounds,
encroaching encroaching—
I can't seem to forget
the look on its face:

fevered red fear
    dry mouth
    open just so
        darting eyes
        slit against the wind

As for the river,
all the while it moseys by—
lazy green currents
carrying people along,
people who float away
before you get to touch them.

IF ONLY

Every creation is derivative,
such as Newton's laws of motion
which stemmed from
Galileo's concept of inertia.

Even though we'd like to be,
not one of us is a bona fide creator—
except, that is, The Magician.
He cuts a woman in two and
then puts her back together.
We all wish we knew how to do that —
how to raise the dead
how to create someone from ashes.

SOUL FOOD

The aroma of homemade bread
doesn't remind me of Mom
because Mom never baked,
seldom even cooked . . .

What reminds me of Mom?
Radio and Redbook and
strangers at the door:

>   godforsaken lonely women
>   who showed up at our house, often—
>   one woman wept by herself, another
>   shuddered and bumped into chairs

In worn high-heeled slippers
and a plaid cotton dress
Mom fixed sandwiches

>   Wonder Bread and Velveeta

serving her waifs
as though they were queens

>   an old silver tray
>   chipped hand-painted china

Little by little
each woman soaked up Mom's laughter,
leaned against her courage

>   grainy, coarse

the texture of homemade bread

THERE USED TO BE SO MANY BUTTERFLIES

◊

When we were each our mother's shadow
fears floated away on kaleidoscope wings:

>tiger swallowtail
>silver spotted skipper

Yesterday dreams hovered
in summer glades where now

>powdery blue ghosts
>flutter aimless
>above asphalt parking lots

◊

For ten cents a dance
Dad waltzed,
his black and gray tweed suit
setting off his salt & pepper hair.

The competition didn't stand a chance
against his black shirt and lemon silk tie.

I rubbed the soft yellow silk against my cheek
every time
before carefully draping it over his tie rack.

◊

In Africa there was a striking
gray black and yellow butterfly
that made a noise like
dried peas in a box.
No one has seen it lately.

CHEF

Every time he made pancakes
Dad made simple syrup:
one cup sugar
one cup water
boil five minutes
let cool.

Dad always knew how to cook, that's why
they put him in charge of the chow wagon,
sent him to the front lines.

Nothing in the world could top
Dad's silver dollar pancakes
with simple syrup,
except maybe his fried potatoes
and shit-on-a-shingle
made with whole milk—not
powdered milk like
he had to use in Belgium.

>Those youngsters had to eat
>so they'd have the strength to
>kill all those other youngsters.

After dessert one time
(Dad made a helluva fried apple pie)
I asked him to compare
his war
to the Vietnam war—
He looked right through me
as though he did not hear.

THIS IS NOT THAT

I didn't mind that Uncle Jimmy's pipe smoke
tickled my nose, or that his faithful bird dog
Queenie snored—although it did and she did.
The way I saw it, Uncle Jimmy could do no wrong
because his lean craggy deep-tanned face was kind.

And when I was seven years old and spotted his
battered truck rumbling back from quail hunting,
I'd race out and jump onto the running board and
he'd hold up the birds for me to see, his smiling
eyes crinkling, just like they always did.

And when I worried about Mom being real sick,
Uncle Jimmy said if you have to worry,
worry that something good will happen,
worry that all heck is going to break loose and
turn into something else, like happiness.

Aunt Betty fried the quail in bacon grease and
served it with hot biscuits and garden green beans.
I was smacking, gobbling down biscuits & honey
when Uncle Jimmy grinned and said:
Tomorrow your mom gets out of the hospital!

I stared at him, dumbfounded, swallowed my
biscuit in a gulp, and then laughed and
jumped around shouting Hooray! Hooray!
But later, when I was packing my stuff—
I felt a shadow of sadness pass over the glee
of going home with Mom the next morning.

And sure enough
for the longest time, right after supper
when I'd be scraping the dishes for Mom
I'd get a whiff of cherry pipe smoke, and hear
a dog, somewhere a long way off, snoring.

WOMAN IN BOTTLE

Aunt Fannie was a sweetheart:
compassionate, fun, an intellectual

Inside the empty whiskey bottle
she lay barely breathing
vacant eyed and vacant

Though by and by, to her rescue
another bottle
full of amber fire and promise

released her—
jettisoned by ethanol energy
into higher and higher momentum

freed her—
exhilarated
accelerated into lightness of being

her skin-tight red dress ajive
in ragtime
in all the smoky bars in Tulsa

jiving teasing drinking swaying
flirting drinking s l u r r I n g
drinking stumbling f
                   a
                    l
                    l
                   i
                n
            g

DAD IS WANING

He hugged me, quick tight often
and gave me a gardenia corsage
for any occasion—every time saying
Twirl around, let me get a look at you
every time telling me I looked like
I'd just stepped out of a bandbox

I was beautiful
because he said so

Now I recall those dress-up days

> untie the satin ribbon from
> round the white corsage box

> slip the velvet cream petals
> out of their cellophane

> inhale luscious perfume

As the days passed oh so swiftly
the wafting scent mellowed
became sickly sweet
my flower of flowers
shriveled, on its way to seed

CERTAINTY

Frida Kahlo shaking her communist fist
was a lot like Grandma
who hated FDR, whose name
you bloody well better not mention—
for killing her Billy Merle, decorated son.

It is good to be
cocksure
about what you despise.

Between revolutions, over and over
Frida painted portraits of her beautiful self,
wild pet monkey perched on her shoulder
nudged beneath her glorious high cheekbone,
like Grandma's.

Those who bulldoze hack char
toucans squawking
jaguars skittish
            are blind to the beauty of Earth,
            wild monkey on her shoulder
I too can squawk and screech—
damn certain
who my enemies are.

AFRICAN DANCERS

Spellbound
by the long-stemmed roses in their teeth
you watch barefoot women dance
for love of loam and seeds and roots.

Hips wrapped in blue & cream damask
swing sway to the drum,
satin lustrous arms clap out the beat,
vivacious laughter carries on the wind.

Too soon
they disappear over the horizon,
drumbeat fading.

You stand and stare into the distance.
You want to know
how these women can laugh
with pale pink roses in their teeth.

You run after them,
want them to come back and
teach you how to do it.

You make the mistake of
searching for them
in all the old familiar places.

LARGESSE

The bag lady *knew it*—
she bought a six-pack of cola
for the gal from out of town
who had tracks up her arms.

Grandma *knew it*—
she helped support the
pregnant divorcée next door
through secretarial school.

All of us are kin
No questions asked
No fingers pointed

At a café table the divorcée
promises to give the baby
to a nervous young couple
who can't agree on anything
but are sure they will be
great parents.

The addict shoots up, opens
the cola can with her teeth,
hums rock-a-bye-baby
as she leans against
the cardboard wall
of her refrigerator crate.

WOODLAND

Take a morning stroll in the woods and
inside you will find, among pale green
quaking aspen and silvery blue spruce,
a basswood felled by lightning, its
stump a thing of awkward beauty

       lichened in bronze
         fringed scalloped ripples
          delicate mushrooms

and something will dart from its center—
       a deer mouse
off to scatter wildflower seeds:

       birdsfoot trefoil, queen anne's lace
         wild ginger, dutchman's breeches
           veronica, wild trout lily, columbine

Trees mice seeds wildflowers
beside an expanding suburb.
We know where
lightning will strike next.

GERMAN WIDOW

Keep at it, work hard—never mind
the corn won't grow above knee-high
on this godforsaken land.

Every Sunday
the Reverend upholds longsuffering.

Four clothespins decorate the pocket
of her plaid jacket; her coveralls cover up
varicose veins as she walks the beans, and
thistles add scratches to her scratched boots.

She stops, straightens, waves across the
field to her neighbor Widower Beverdorf
who takes a bath most Saturdays—
he likes getting dandied up for a dance
with the plump pretty teacher in town.

Teachers don't speak broken English
or have sun wrinkles round their eyes
or calloused fingers—but then again
neither can they
pitch out of the loft the cows some hay.

If only
she had someone to whisper to in church.

LAS VEGAS

He and his hound dog Mac lost
the car at the craps table,
with nothing for it but to walk home,
though sometimes a trucker was glad to
pick up a man and his dog and suitcase and
carry them as far as his next turn-off.

Unfortunately,
there wasn't much traffic as
he and Mac walked Route 66
through the Mojave Desert—
both of them desperate for water.

And there it was at the end—Water
to drink and to get his socks off, his sister
clucking as she pulled at submerged
crusty threads stuck to oozing blisters.
Mac's pads were cracked, but he healed
fast, bounding here and there.

When her brother healed too,
his sister silently hoped
next time the two would settle
for a trip downtown and back.
Hope is such a terrible thing.

OSTRICH

The proper place to ride an ostrich is
not necessarily in scorching South Africa.

She decided to do it because now behold
she's retired, and has time, and a yen—

A sudden summer storm lashes at the
Rocky Mountain Ostrich Festival:
Wind-driven rain in heavy sheets makes her grip
slippery on the stumpy half-wings meant
as her brace. The panicked behemoth,
amazingly swift in its lumbering gait,
zigzags through thunder and lightning to
rid itself of the thing on its back.

By the grace of the universe she lasts two seconds,
vainly grasping at oily feathers for leverage before
sliding sideways and off, landing spread eagle
face-up in mud and downpour, befuddled to see
matted water-soaked plumes fanning above her
and talons stomping her ribs in slow motion. She
shouts above the storm to tell this poor dumb anomaly
that she too is of the Stone Age, that they are kin—
but then it's over, and two extant misfits, drenched and
shivering, gasp and struggle to catch their breath.

......

Inside the festival lodge, swaddled, huddled beside
a cozy fire, she winces from the pain of broken ribs—
Oh my, it hurts so much when she shakes with laughter,
bent over, clutching her midriff, tears unstoppable at
the thought of herself shouting through the rain trying
to explain to a seven-foot bird that she understands
how fear can now and again possess you.

A HABIT

Gathering pinecones for the students' wreath project, I'm careful to select only the perfect. A squirrel darts up a tree and reminds me of our friend Martin—of how he loved to watch squirrels scamper about, his face lit by a crooked smile, drool running out the corner of his mouth onto the arm of his wheelchair.

I think of the time at the state fair when he spilled soda all over his lap, and his slow, measured words, "Oh – well – most - of – it – just – runs – down – my – chin – anyway!" Grinning hugely at his own humor, he swiped with his good arm at the sticky soda, making matters worse and causing him and us to laugh even harder.

I stop discarding broken, limp pinecones—but by and by my mind wanders and I catch myself again selecting only the perfect. I make a renewed effort not to. I repeat this process over and over until finally the burlap bag is full.

EL SALVADOR

1981 through 2021

They say Isabella crossed herself
before she took the moldy cheese
from her rich employer's garbage, to
make pupusas for her family's supper

Sunset
streaked with the blood
of freedom's ghosts

They say the child Juanita
unrolled her straw mat
on the powdery dirt floor
and slept a fitful gnawing

Sunrise
morning harbinger
of more missing peasants
The Disappeared

They say Mamá Umana picking
through the village dump for food
came upon a severed tongue
and a man's hacked-off leg

2022

They say Mamá Elena picking
through the village dump for food
came upon a hacked-off leg, on which
were her son's pant leg and shoe

They say Alejandra crosses herself
before she takes the moldy cheese
from her *very rich* employer's garbage,
to make pupusas for her family's supper

They say the child Marina
unrolls her straw mat
on the powdery dirt floor
and sleeps a fitful gnawing

Stand strong with your bare feet on the ground

and with everything that comes from it.

Be smarter every day by listening to your intuition,

looking at the world with your forehead...

and always remember,

you are the medicine.

Wisdom: María Sabina, Mexican Healer and Poet

"What day is it?" asked Winnie-the-Pooh

"It's today," squeaked Piglet

"My favorite day," said Pooh

A.A. Milne